HOW TO
CHANGE THE WORLD
in 12 easy steps

Inspired by the life lessons of Eva Mozes Kor

by Peggy Porter Tierney
illustrations by Marie Letourneau

Tanglewood | Indianapolis

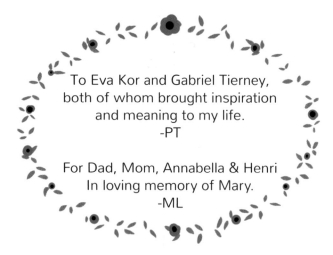

To Eva Kor and Gabriel Tierney,
both of whom brought inspiration
and meaning to my life.
-PT

For Dad, Mom, Annabella & Henri
In loving memory of Mary.
-ML

The publisher would like to thank Beth Nairn for her creative input.

Published by Tanglewood Publishing, Inc.
© 2021 Peggy Porter Tierney and Marie Letourneau

Cover and Interior Design by Marie Letourneau

Tanglewood Publishing, Inc. | 1060 N. Capitol Ave., Ste. E-395 | Indianapolis, IN 46204 | www.tanglewoodbooks.com

Printed in U.S.A.
10 9 8 7 6 5 4 3 2 1

ISBN 978-1-939100-54-2

Library of Congress Cataloging-in-Publication Data
Names: Tierney, Peggy, author. | Le Tourneau, Marie, illustrator.
Title: How to change the world in 12 easy steps / by Peggy Porter Tierney ; illustrations by Marie Letourneau.
Description: Indianapolis, IN : Tanglewood, 2021. | Audience: Ages 4 & up | Audience: Grades K-1 | Summary: "How to Change the World in 12 Easy Steps was inspired by Eva Kor,
a child survivor of Auschwitz. She always stressed to young audiences that even though a child, they had the power to change the world. Easy, simple gestures from picking up a
piece of trash on the sidewalk, tidying a bedroom, accepting someone who is different, along with other gestures of kindness and thoughtfulness can make a big difference. The book could also
serve as a starting point for a conversation on prejudice. Marie Letourneau's illustrations capture the warmth at the heart of this book, making it a fun, but life-changing read"-- Provided by publisher.
Identifiers: LCCN 2021026585 (print) | LCCN 2021026586 (ebook) | ISBN 9781939100542 (hardcover) | ISBN 9781939100559 (ebook)
Subjects: LCSH: Forgiveness--Juvenile literature. | Kindness--Juvenile literature. | Thoughtfulness--Juvenile literature. | Kor, Eva Mozes.
Classification: LCC BF637.F67 T54 2021 (print) | LCC BF637.F67 (ebook) | DDC 155.9/2--dc23
LC record available at https://lccn.loc.gov/2021026585
LC ebook record available at https://lccn.loc.gov/2021026586

Did you know you have the power
to change the world?

It's easier than you think.

Start small.
Make your bed and tidy your room.

Give your parents a kiss and a hug.

If you see a piece of trash, throw it away.

If you see someone who needs help, volunteer to help them.

Smile at someone.

Do you see someone sitting alone?
Invite them to join you or go sit with them.

Is someone being bullied?

Stand up to the bully with them. But don't bully the bully.

Everyone is different. Accept people for who they are.

Just be the best *you* that you can be.

Stay in school and develop your beautiful mind.

Never give up on yourself or your dreams. All things in life are possible.

Forgive people who hurt you or your feelings. Forgiveness doesn't mean that what they did was okay or that you have to be friends. It is important to stay safe from people if they might hurt you again.

Forgiveness means that you decide you don't want to be angry, and when the anger is gone, there is more space for happiness. It might take some time to be ready to forgive, and that is okay.

This book is based on beliefs and teachings
of a woman named Eva Kor.

eva & miriam.

When she was a child, Eva and her family were put into
a prison camp, where her parents and older sisters died.

Many years later, Eva met a doctor who worked at the camp where her family died. The doctor was very kind and gave her help she asked for. She decided writing him a letter of forgiveness would be the best way for her to thank him. Eva then decided to forgive all of the people who caused her so much pain. To her surprise, forgiveness gave her feelings of power and happiness, and she wanted to tell everyone about her experience.

Eva spoke all over the world about her life and her beliefs to many adult audiences, from local teachers to world leaders. But above all, Eva cared most about speaking to children. She wanted every child to know that with small gestures and forgiveness, they could change the world.

Eva was right. Even if you are young, you have the power to be kind, to be happy and to make people around you more kind and happy. Always remember: making the world a better place can start with one person - and that person is YOU.